Dear Parents,

Thank you for purchasing our book. We are thrilled to be part of your child's reading journey. By choosing this book, you have taken an important first step in improving your child's reading skills.

To make the most out of this book, we recommend reading one to two stories a day for about thirty minutes. Feel free to break this session into two parts if needed to keep your child engaged and focused. After reading, encourage your child to color the picture that accompanies each story. This not only makes learning fun but also reinforces what they have just read.

We understand that starting a new reading program can feel overwhelming, but remember that consistency is key. Setting aside dedicated reading time each day will help build a strong routine and foster a love for reading in your child. If you're unsure where to start, focusing on vowel sounds in order we have provided is a great approach. This foundational skill is crucial for developing strong reading abilities and will give your child the confidence they need to progress.

Additionally, creating a comfortable and distraction-free reading environment can make a significant difference. Choose a quiet spot where your child can concentrate, and make sure they have all the materials they need, including crayons for coloring. Positive reinforcement and praise can also motivate your child and make the learning experience enjoyable.

Should you need any guidance or a FREE placement test, please don't hesitate to email us. We are here to support you and your child every step of the way. Our goal is to provide you with the tools and resources necessary to make reading a positive and rewarding experience.

Thank you once again for your support. Together, we can make a significant difference in your child's reading journey. Your commitment and involvement play a crucial role in their success, and we are honored to be a part of this important milestone.

Warm regards,
Budding Brains Books

TABLE OF CONTENTS

Vowel Team
ai

Gail has a snail. It is on a trail. She feeds it grain. A boy, Dean, has a cat. The cat likes to play. Gail and Dean sit by the lake. They see a boat with a sail. The snail and cat wait. Gail and Dean eat a meal. They share bread. The day is good. They have a great time by the lake.

Nate has a pail. He takes it to the lake. His pal, Gail, has paint. They paint rocks by the trail. A snail moves by the pail. Gail paints the snail. Nate and Gail wait for the paint to dry. The sun is hot. They play all day. When the paint is dry, they smile. They had a great time by the lake.

Vowel Team
ay and ey

Ray and Kay play in the hay. They stay all day. The sun is hot and the sky is blue. They run and play by the bay. A grey cat hops in the fun. Kay feeds it some hay. Ray makes a clay toy. They all sit and rest. The day is warm and they feel happy. They wave and say, "What a fun day!"

Jay and May play by the bay. They stay all day. The sky is grey, but they don't mind. They find a stray cat and give it hay. The cat is happy and stays. Jay and May make a clay toy. They have fun in the sand. The day turns warm and sunny. They wave and say, "What a great day!"

Vowel Teams Long A- All Combinations

Jay has eight big meals on his tray. One was a nice, big steak. Jay aims to eat it all. He says, "This steak may be the best yet!" As he lays his fork and knife by the plate, he sees the light gray sky by the pane. He sighs, feeling great joy. Today, Jay stays in to enjoy his day with a tasty piece of steak.

Kay and Ray find a big pie by a tree. They see it has eight thin slices. Kay says, "This pie may be sweet! Let's try it." Ray gets a tray and lays the pie on it. They each take a slice. "Yay, I like this pie!" says Kay with a smile. The pie is all gone in a short time. They play by the tree the rest of the day.

Sam and Ray take a flight to Spain. They stay in the plane and play games. They watch the rain and the gray clouds sway away. When they land, they say, "Yay!" Sam takes a tray and lays out some fruit. They share a grape, and both say, "This day is great!"

Ray has a big tray of grain. Each day, he takes it to the bay to play. He lays the tray in the sun and the grain gets dry. One day, a jay flies by and sees the grain. The jay stays by the tray and eats the grain. Ray does not mind. The jay says, "Thank you!" with each peck. Ray smiles and enjoys his day by the bay.

Jay and Kai find a pail. They fill it with gray paint. They play and spray the paint on a big tray. The day is bright, they may paint away. The tray is light. They paint the tray red, then gray. The tray is neat and they feel gay. They say, "Yay!" as they play and paint all day.

Kay has long hair. She likes a nice braid. One day, she may play with clay. She will lay the clay on a tray. Then, she will braid her hair. The braid is gray. It is not plain. It may sway as she plays. Kay feels gay with her braid all day. She says, "This braid is my best one, yay!"

One sunny day, May and Fay went to play by the bay. They laid a big, gray mat on the sand. May had a pail and spade to dig. Fay had a sail for his toy boat. Then, they ate snacks on the mat. They had a great day at the bay. May and Fay plan to come again.

Ray and Mai take a ride on a train one day. They pay the fare and find a seat by a big window. The train sways as it speeds away. They play a game and say the names they see on signs. They wave goodbye when the train stops. What a fine day for a ride!

Vowel Team
Long E-
ee and ea

Lee and Pete see a green tree. They feel the cool breeze. Pete eats a peach, and Lee eats a sweet treat. They hear bees buzz near the tree. They see a deer by the creek. Lee and Pete cheer. They play by the tree and share their treats. The day is warm and bright. They had fun and feel happy. It was a great day.

Sheep see a bee by the creek. The bee lands on a green leaf. Pete and Eve feed the sheep. They give them wheat and peas. The sun is high, and the breeze is cool. Pete and Eve play near the creek. They splash and laugh. The sheep rest in the shade. It is a sweet and fun day by the creek.

Vowel Team Long E- ei and ie

Brie and Neil like to hike. They see a big, green field. Brie finds a pie in her pack. They sit by a tree to eat. Neil sees a deer near the field. The deer is quiet and shy. Brie and Neil smile and wave. The sun is high, and the sky is blue. They have a fun day in the field.

Chief Pete and his niece, Sheila, like to be weird. They tie a red kite to a tree. They eat pie with beans. Sheila sees a green beetle. Chief Pete feels the cool breeze. They smile with glee. Pete wears a silly hat. Sheila sings a funny song. They laugh all day. It is a bright, fun time. Chief Pete and Sheila enjoy being weird.

Vowel Team Long E-ey

Riley has a pet donkey. They walk in the alley. The donkey finds a piece of honey. Riley gives it some money. They see a monkey in a tree. The day is sunny and bright. They walk to the valley. Riley finds a shiny penny. The donkey is happy. They sit and rest. Riley loves the donkey. It is a fun day beyond the alley.

Riley and Casey walk in the valley. They see a grey turkey. It finds honey and eats. Riley gives it a tiny penny. They see a monkey by the tree. The day is sunny and warm. They walk down the alley. Casey finds a shiny toy. Riley and Casey smile. They pet the donkey and play. It is a fun day beyond the alley.

Vowel Team Long E- All Combinations

In a deep green field, a seed lay beneath the soil. One sunny day, Steve the bee flew by and saw the seed peek out. The seed felt shy but keen to grow. With each ray of sunshine and every drop of rain, the seed grew. Soon, it was a tall tree! Steve came by again and cheered.

Lee has a bean. He keeps the bean by a tree. Lee digs deep and plants the bean. He feels the need to feed it. Each week, he frees weeds and feeds the bean. One day, he peeks and sees a green leaf. The bean is three feet high! Lee feels joy. He yells, "Hey, see my bean, it's neat!"

Jay has big feet. He sees them each day. He feels weird, but he is keen to play. His feet are not like any we see. Jay meets a bee by a tree. The bee flies by Jay's knee. "Nice feet," says the bee. Jay smiles with glee. His feet, all big, help him be free. Jay and his feet live happily.

Lee the sheep feels keen to see the green meadow. He peeks between the trees and sees bees near the creek. Lee leaps and bleats, "Yippee!" He meets three deer and they cheer. Lee spies sweet berries. He eats and enjoys the treat. "What a fine, sunny day," says Lee, feeling merry.

Eve sees a big deer near the green trees. Eve keeps meat and cheese by the jeep. The deer peeks and smells the meat. It seems pleased. Eve says, "Here, have some meat!" The deer eats and seems happy. Eve then sits and enjoys the breeze, watching the deer leap away.

Lee and Bea have a meal by the sea. Bea peels a sweet pear while Lee fries beef. They share cheese and drink tea. Then, they eat cake and pie. The meal is nice and the day is sunny. Lee and Bea enjoy their feast and feel at ease. They leave the sea with glee.

In a green field, a tall weed stood near a tree. Bees flew freely, keen to feel the breeze. The weed felt weak as sheep came near. One sheep tried to eat the weed, but it was too sleek. The sheep bleated. The weed, feeling brave, kept its seeds safe. It swayed gently in the peaceful day.

Vowel Team
Long I

Liam the lion likes to lie high on a bright hill. He sighs with glee as he spies the light blue sky. One night, Liam finds a big, ripe pie by his side. He tries to bite the pie, but sighs. Then, he ties the pie to his side and flies up high into the sky.

One fine day, a big fly with bright wings took flight in the high sky. It went by a wide pine. The fly liked to glide and dive. With each slide in the sky, it felt pride. It flew high and nigh, past the light of the sun. Then, it spied a pie on a sill. "This pie will be mine," it said with a grin.

In the bright light, Mike finds a tie with a high, tight fit. He likes this tie since it shines with rich, ripe hues. Mike ties it right, sighing with pride. With the tie flapping wide, he rides by the white signs. Mike smiles wide, his tie still tight and fine.

Rick rides his bike at night. He likes to see the bright light shine from his bike. The high hills are hard to climb, but Rick tries with all his might. Rick spots a kite flying high in the sky. It flies right by him. What a sight to see! Rick feels free as he rides back home with glee.

Lily likes to fly her kite high in the sky. She ties a line to the kite and lets it rise. The kite flies up with a sigh. It dips and zips, high and then low. She pulls the line tight, and the kite dips right. High in the sky, the kite is a bright sight!

Clyde is a bright child who likes to hike high hills with his kite. One fine night, he saw a light shine right by the sight of his white kite. He tried to fight the fright he felt and sighed when he found it was just the moonlight. Now, every time Clyde flies his kite, he hopes to see the cool light on his nighttime hike.

Tim had a big pie. He set the pie on his dish and sat by the side. The pie had a high pile of rich, ripe figs on top. Tim had a big grin as he bit into the pie. It was the best pie he had! Tim gave his pig a tiny bit of pie. Tim and his pig had a fine time with the big, rich pie.

Jill likes to ride her car at night. This time, she rides by the wide lake. The sight of the white waves makes her smile. Jill thinks it might be time to dine on some pie, so she rides back home fast. Her big sister Kate has made a nice lime pie. They sit and enjoy the pie together

Vowel Team Long O- All Combinations

Joe had a new bow. It was a high bow with a red glow. He took it to the park to show Mo, his pal. The sun was hot, so they sat below a big oak. Joe put the bow on his lap and told Mo how he got it. They set up a row of cans and Joe let the bow go. The cans fell down in a row. Mo clapped and said, "Go Joe!"

Poe is an old man who loves to stroll down a long road near his home. Poe keeps walking until he spots a crow on a low branch. The crow caws loudly, and Poe laughs. He finds an oak tree and sits below it, watching the clouds flow by. Poe feels calm, enjoying the slow day.

Zoe rows her boat slow. She sees a toad on a road and waves. The toad hops slow to the side. Zoe floats to a cove. She has a map to show a spot to go. She rows on. The wind now blows, and the boat rocks. She rows to a dock. She hops down and finds a glow. "Wow!" Zoe yells. "Gold!"

Mia has a big red bow. She goes to a show with Joe. They row a boat on a slow, wide moat. The oars flow through the cool, blue water. The sun sets low, and the sky glows pink and gold. Mia and Joe row back as the stars show. Mia's bow still sits atop her head, bold and bright.

Tom has toast at home. He likes to load lots of jam on each slice with some oatmeal. The jam flows down the sides. One day, Tom drops his toast on the floor. He knows he cannot eat it now. Tom is sad, but he goes to make more toast and oatmeal. Soon, he is glad again as he takes a big bite of his jammy toast.

One day, a toad named Joe hops down to a coast. The coast is calm and full of hope. Joe spots some fish and tries to leap on a big, slow one. "No, no," says the fish as it goes away. Joe floats low in the cool mud. "Oh, so slow!" he moans. He now knows to wait and go slow.

Joe and Zoe go to a show. On the road, they see snow flow past the window. Zoe says, "Oh no, look at the snow!" They stop by a row of oak trees. The snow is deep. Joe and Zoe throw snowballs. Soon, they go home, slow and cold. They sip hot cocoa to warm up from the snow.

In a lush, cool grove, a doe roams alone. She stops to sip from a slow, deep brook. With a leap, she hops onto the road. The doe spots a crow on a high bough. "Go slow!" crows the bird, as the doe nods. Soon, she finds oats near a low oak. What a joy! She chews the sweet meal, then dozes off in the shade.

Long Vowel
U- ew

Drew has a new blue hat. He likes to show it to his friends. Sue sees the hat and smiles. She wants a hat, too. They walk to the park and play by the pond. Drew and Sue see a few ducks. The sun is bright, and the sky is clear. They feel happy. Drew's new hat looks cool. They had a fun day with the new hat.

Luke and Beth have a new puppy. The puppy is cute and loves to chew. Luke gives it a blue toy. The puppy chews and plays. Beth gets a few more toys. The puppy is happy and wags its tail. They knew the puppy needed love. Luke and Beth laugh and play. The day is bright and full of joy. The puppy feels at home.

Long Vowel
Team U- ue

Sue and Luke have a blue canoe. They take it to the lake. The sky is clear and blue. They use a map to find a clue. The clue leads them to a cave. Inside, they see a big blue glue. Sue and Luke feel happy. They knew the gem was true. They take the gem back in the canoe. It was a fun day for Sue and Luke.

Sue and Jake went to the venue. They saw a blue clue on the wall. It was true and gave them a clue to the next game. Sue used some glue to fix a toy. Jake made sure they had fuel for the car. They walked down the avenue. A dog needed rescue. They helped it and felt good. The day had value. Sue and Jake were happy and kind.

Long Vowel U- All Combinations

Jude got a new flute. It was a gift from his aunt Sue. The flute had a gleam like the moon. Jude blew into the flute. The tune was sweet and flew like a tune in the wind. Each note drew Jude in. He knew he would play this flute each day at dusk.

Luke had a red ruby. He kept it in a box. The gem was very rare. Each day, Luke would view it with joy. He knew the ruby had a deep hue that few could find. The ruby shone like a new fire. It made Luke feel like a true king in his small den.

Cupid flew to brew a stew. He knew just what to do. He threw peas, leeks, and beef into the pot. As the stew grew, he drew a heart in dew. "Who will chew this stew?" Cupid mused. Soon, two who knew Cupid came. They ate the stew and felt love anew.

Sue had a blue tulip in a cute jug. The jug was on a new rug in her room. Sue took good care of her tulip. Each day, she gave it dew to keep it wet. The sun shone on it from the pane. The tulip grew tall and true. Sue knew her love made it bloom.

June has a mule. The mule can bray and chew, but June has a new plan. She plays a tune on her flute. The mule must like the tune, as it sits near June. They stay by a huge tree and feel free. The tune and the mule make a cute duo.

Luke has a blue cube. He uses the cube to muse on hues. Luke puts the cube on a dune to view. The sun glows, and the blue cube shows new hues. It is like a clue in a hue stew. Luke feels glad to have the blue cube.

A blue tuna swam deep in the sea. He knew he must flee when he saw a huge new net. The crew on the ship drew the net. The tuna swam to the blue reef. He blew past the seaweed. Safe now, the tuna grew calm as he swam through the deep blue sea.

Rue and Jules went to the cafe to get some stew. They sat at the blue table. Rue had stew with peas, and Jules had stew with beef. Rue used a new spoon to eat her stew. She said the stew was good. The peas were huge and soft. Jules took a few sips and let out a big smile. They had a nice meal.

FREE RESOURCES

If you want free resources,

please email

buddingbrainsbooksllc@gmail.com

to get access to our free

giveaways and strategy guides.

TEACHER GRATITUDE

Write a letter to a teacher who has had a memorable impact on your educational journey so far.

_____

_____

_____

_____

_____

_____

_____

_____

_____

41590341R00039